MW00962124

DON'T LET HER LEAD

How To Take Back Control Of Your Relationship And Become The Man Your Woman Needs And Craves

Zak Roedde

Copyright © 2021 Zak Roedde

All rights reserved

No part of this book may be reproduced, or stored in a retrieval system, or transmitted in any form or by any means, electronic, mechanical, photocopying, recording, or otherwise, without express written permission of the publisher.

ISBN- 9798599459385

CONTENTS

CONTENTS

INTRODUCTION

Relationships are supposed to be amazing. Every day should be filled with passion, love, connection, humor, and conflict-free enjoyment of each other. Imagine a relationship where you are always attracted to your woman, and she is always attracted to you. You both love spending time with each other. You never have conflicts or arguments and everything works smoothly. Your woman never burdens you, and everything you do for her feels like a joy. You are free to do whatever you want, but what you want is to become the best man you can for her and make her as happy as possible.

I am not talking about the first few months of a relationship. This is a dynamic that is not only sustainable, but it actually gets *better* the longer you stay together. I'm experiencing such a relationship right now, and many of my male clients are seeing the same results as they do their own work. And it is possible for *you* to experience this with your woman too.

But only if you don't let her lead.

I have written this book for my past self. It is exactly what I needed to know five years ago before I met my wife. If I had understood the contents of this book back then, I could have saved my wife and I so much suffering and misunderstandings and hurt feelings. But I didn't know it, because I had been indoctrinated with lies and misunderstands about men and women, and how relationship are supposed to work.

I used to believe that men and women should both lead, and

both follow. They should both negotiate. They should both be vulnerable. They should both assert their needs and wants. They should both set boundaries. They should both treat each other the same. I tried my absolute best to make this dynamic work.

But it just doesn't work well. I was wrong. I was embarrassingly wrong.

The man should lead absolutely everything. Every step of the way. And to do that, he must lead his woman to stop leading anything.

He must lead to get her number.

He must lead to ask her on a date.

He must lead all the dates from start to finish.

He must lead with physically escalating up to and including sex.

He must lead by setting the terms in the relationship.

He must lead by setting all expectations.

He must lead by setting all boundaries.

He must lead by guiding any conflict to resolution.

He must lead his woman to her feelings.

He must lead by helping his woman grow.

He must lead by teaching himself to grow.

He must lead by telling his woman what to do.

He must lead by taking care of the finances.

He must lead by deciding the children's care and education.

He must lead by anticipating his woman's needs.

He must lead by deciding how chores and work will be divided.

He must lead by initiating contact.

He must lead everything until the day the relationship ends, from breakup or death.

Does this sound really sexist, unfair, and ridiculous to you? I would have thought the same thing if I was reading this book five years ago, or even two years ago. I might have been tempted to throw it out and read something else. Or burn it. But that was because I didn't understand how men and women are fundamentally different and also perfectly complementary for each other in their strengths and weaknesses.

This complementary nature of men and women is best illustrated by observing a salsa dance. Like most dances, the salsa is performed by the man leading the woman. Every step of the way. At no point does the woman lead the man, not even for a second.

Is the salsa dance sexist? Is the woman dancer considered 'inferior'? Do her needs not matter?

Obviously not, on all counts. In salsa, the woman partner is just as important as the man. Her role is just as necessary. Being a 'follower' is often considered weak in our society, because most followers are mindless drones. But this is not true in salsa. The woman is not 'less' than the man because she is following him. The man is actually leading the salsa dance *for* his woman. He is doing it to give her an amazing experience. A woman allowing a man to give her an amazing experience is not weak. Not in a dance, and not in a relationship. A woman is weak only when she follows a leader who doesn't care about her needs or her experience. But this book is going to show men how to become a devotional leader, the kind of man who leads out of love. The kind of men that self-respecting women love to follow.

Being a 'follower' is often considered easy. And it is true that it is easy to be a bad follower. But it is very difficult to be a good follower, just like it is very difficult to be a good leader. In both salsa and in a relationship. It requires the ability to let go of control and flow with the leader. It requires an incredible amount of trust and communication. In a salsa dance, if the woman tries to take the lead or is resistant to the man's lead, the dance quickly falls apart. It just does not work. Similarly, if the man is passive and doesn't lead, or is not paying attention to how his woman is responding, the dance falls apart.

The same is true in a relationship. A good relationship requires a man who is always leading, and a woman who is always following. With excellent communication so that both partners get their needs met and have an incredible experience. If the woman is not doing a good job following, it means the man is not doing a good job leading. And to become a better leader, he needs to lead his woman to stop leading. He needs to teach her to become a good follower. Because that is what good leaders do.

But why is it that the man leads, and the woman follows, instead of the reverse?

Because it is in our genes. It is hardwired for this to be the natural way relationships function. A woman can lead, and she can learn to become good at it. She may become a better leader than her man, or better than most men. But she will never thrive leading her relationship. She will feel increasingly drained and disconnected from her man. Similarly, a man can follow, and he can learn to become good at it. He may become a better follower than his woman, or better than most women. But he will never thrive following his woman's lead. He will feel increasingly weak and disconnected from his woman.

Whereas when a woman follows her man's lead, she feels safe, free and energized. She can relax and enjoy herself and enjoy being cared for.

When a man leads his woman, he feels powerful, respected and energized. He can become responsible and feel more alive than he has ever felt.

This is exactly what my wife and I experienced when I decided to turn our relationship into a salsa dance. My wife is an extremely confident, assertive, self-respecting woman. She is an incredible leader and has fearlessly led groups in a corporate environment. She has no fear leading me, and has done so. Whereas I am naturally a very passive and anxious follower. I have spent a decade learning how to become a confident leader, but wasn't fully embodying it in my marriage until I realized it was the only way to make it function the way I wanted. It's not about ones current abilities, it is about potential abilities and enjoyment. I thrive leading my wife, and she thrives following me. Whereas I want to kill myself when I was being led by my wife... and I'm pretty sure she wanted to kill me.

Only once I decided to stop letting her lead, did everything transform for the better.

Have you ever played a video-game you really loved? A game where you were in control of everything? A game where you got to plan, and anticipate, and decide? Remember how fun it was to be responsible for all of those things to meet your goals? You had to analyze the situation, make a plan, and execute it. You then had to do it over and over as you learned how to do it better. You had to perfect yourself as a gamer to beat each level and win the game.

Well, you're relationship is the greatest and most fulfilling video-game you will ever play. The goal of your relationship is to maximize the amount of love you can give your woman, which will be multiplied and given back to you when she receives it. Your intent for everything you do is to give her your gift of love. You are playing this game for *her,* but you *both* end up winning.

How do you achieve your goal and win the game? Four words: DON'T LET HER LEAD!

LEADING AND FOLLOWING
(TRAINING LEVEL)

If you let your woman lead, you start losing the game. Your relationship will becoming increasingly impaired. The more you allow your woman to lead, the more you will suffer. The less your woman will respect you. The less interest you will have in devoting to your woman. And the less attraction and connection you will feel for each other. The greatest gift you can give your woman is don't let her lead.

But to give her that gift, you have to understand what it looks like and feels like when a woman is leading. Leading is far more than just telling a man 'Go do the dishes." Sometimes it is that obvious, and if your woman is leading in that very obvious way, that is a huge problem that must be immediately stopped. But rarely is it that obvious. If it was always that obvious, it would be very easy to stop and you wouldn't need an entire book on the subject. All you would need is to grow some balls. But it is almost never that obvious.

A person is 'leading' by my definition whenever they are trying to get an *outcome*. That outcome is getting their partner to 'do' something. If a woman *tries* to get her man to give her approval or avoid disapproval, she is leading to get an outcome. If a woman *tries* to make her man happy, or make him unhappy, she is leading to get an outcome. If a woman *tries* to get her man to meet any of her wants or needs, she is leading to get an outcome. If a woman *tries* to get her man to stop doing something she doesn't like, she is leading to get an outcome. If a woman *tries* to get her man to do *anything,* she is leading to get an outcome. And you as her man must put a stop to it.

That does not mean I advocate that a woman stay a silent doormat all the time as her needs and wants go unmet, and her feelings and boundaries are trampled upon. That would be a very unhealthy relationship which would be unfulfilling for both partners. Instead, I advocate for women learning how to only express for the sake of expressing. And it is your job to teach her how to do that.

Everyone who is artistically inclined will understand this. All musicians, painters, sculptors, dancers, and writers. They understand that there are two reasons to create their art.

The first reason is to get an outcome. They create their art with the intent of making money, getting attention, acquiring fans, becoming famous, or helping people. There is nothing wrong with trying to get any of these outcomes. I call this 'leading'. I am writing this book and part of my intent in doing so is to hopefully get all of those outcomes, that would be fantastic!

The second reason is to not get an outcome. It's to create their art because they want to express what is inside of them. They want to express who they are and how they feel, regardless of what happens, good or bad. Creating art for this reason is not 'right' or 'wrong'. It just 'is'. It is 'submitting' to what is, and what may be, without trying to effect the outcome. I call this 'expressing'.

Similarly, a woman can act to try to get an outcome from her man, or she can submit to what is and express what is inside of her without trying to effect anything.

If she isn't spending enough time with her man, she can:

Try to lead her man to an outcome she wants by saying "Hey

let's spend some time together."

Or she can:

Express what is inside of her, without trying to get any outcome at all."I feel lonely."

The difference between these two examples may not seem like a big deal. But it is a very big deal. Even for men who do not yet realize that it is a big deal.

Whenever a woman leads a man in any way, she is communicating two things:

1.   She is communicating that she doesn't trust her man to take care of her needs if she were to just express herself without trying to get an outcome.

2.   She is communicating that she isn't worthy of her needs being met if she were to just express herself without putting the effort in to assert herself.

A woman tries to lead to get an outcome because she doesn't believe she can get one without asserting herself in some way. Without *trying* to get her man to do something. If a man continues to passively allow his woman to lead him in this way, he is doing her a huge disservice. His passivity will mean that she will never gain that trust in him, and gain that self-worth in herself. She will always believe that she will have to exert herself to get the love that she needs. But a man's passivity does far more harm than that!

A man needs to be able to lead his relationship. When his woman is fully respecting his leadership, he feels respected as a man. He feels compelled to devote to his woman and meet her needs and make her happy, because he feels like 'the man'. But if he does not feel respected, his desire to devote to his woman will become stifled. A man only feels joy from devoting to his woman if it is through his leadership. If he is devoting through his submission to her leadership, he will feel no joy at all. He will feel turned off, disrespected, and disconnected from his woman. That means every time he passively allows his woman to lead, he allows her to hurt him, and thus he indirectly allows her to hurt herself.

But worse than that, when a man lets his woman lead, he stifles his own growth as a man. When a man is able to lead fully and is inspired to become the best man he can be for his woman, the sky is the limit. He will work diligently to become more grounded, more focused, more loving, more ambitious, more accepting, more powerful, more of a man in every way that his woman needs. A man's love for his woman is one of the most powerful motivations he can possibly have to better himself. But if she leads, it enables laziness and apathy. That means your growth as a man is dependent on your woman getting out of your way. Which means you need to lead her to get out of your way!

But guess what?

It's still even far worse than *that!* Because unlike a man, a woman really doesn't like leading. She will hate leading her man. She will hate telling him to do things. She will hate being in control. A woman may feel compelled to lead because she has a fear of *not* being in control. She may feel compelled to lead because she thinks she has to if she wants to be respected as a woman. She may feel compelled to lead because she has been conditioned to believe that a woman leading in a relationship is healthy and empowering. But she doesn't enjoy it. When she leads, she loses attraction for her man. She loses interest in becoming intimate with him. She loses interest in sex. She becomes increasingly guarded, neurotic, stressed, and unhappy. There is literally nothing good about a woman leading her man.

So don't let her lead, as a gift to her. If you care about your woman and love her, don't let her lead. It may not be easy to stop her from leading, but you must find a way if you love her, and want to stay with her. You must make that your goal in your relationship, and you must take it very seriously. Every time you fail in that goal and let your woman lead, you are hurting her. And you are hurting yourself.

You must have a solid inner-vision for your relationship. An idea of what it should look like in your ideal world. The ideal inner-vision for your relationship is where you are always in the leadership role trying to get outcomes which make both you and your woman happy. Your woman is in the submissive (follower) role, allowing you to lead, and expressing how your leadership makes her feel. This creates a giving-receiving dynamic. You give your leadership, she receives it. Just like the salsa dance.

For this dynamic to work, you must lead her to stop leading you. But to do that, you need to see all of the subtle ways that she is leading you. Ways that you are not even consciously aware of. You are only subconsciously aware of them. Your body knows if you are being led, and it is always telling you by making you feel slightly irritated or demotivated from acting when your woman expresses something to get an outcome. This is in stark contrast to when your woman is not leading in any way and treating you with full respect as a man. This will make you feel alive and joyful to meet her needs and make her feel happy. Learn to feel into your body when your woman is interacting with you, and learn to trust what it is telling you. I can give you conceptual understanding of why your body is telling you things, but it's your body that needs to be listened to most of the time.

Unless you want to pay me hundreds of dollars an hour to coach you every minute of the day? I am a relationship coach, so I am open to that too. But I'm not cheap. Listening to your body is the better budget option.

One of the most obvious ways that your body will tell you that your woman is leading is when she gives you a solution to something. She is telling you what she wants you to do. She is trying to get an outcome, and the outcome is the solution that she offered. That will not feel good.

"I'd love it if we could go out to get food tonight."

"I'd like some help with the dishes."

"I want to spend some time alone with you tonight."

"Let's have sex!"

OK that last solution might feel good to hear, but only if it was something you really wanted at the time.

All of the above are solutions, and when a woman offers them, she is trying to get that solution as an outcome. By offering them and leading you, she prevents you from coming up with your own solution and leading her. You will have little to no desire to do what she wants, unless it was something you really wanted to do anyway. Because now your only choice she has given you is to say 'no' or submit to her leadership.

"I'm getting bored of eating at home all the time."

"I'm too tired to do the dishes."

"I miss you."

"I feel horny."

These are all problems. And a woman is just expressing them for the sake of expressing them when she states these problems without trying to get any outcome. She is submitting to what is, and leaving it up to you to create a solution and lead towards it. You will have a strong desire to solve the problem for her and make her happy, even if it wasn't something you wanted to do. You will feel like her hero coming to her rescue and saving her from the problem. Because your greatest need in your relationship is to lead your woman with devotion to make her happy. Right?

OK, it is possible that you are not yet aware that it is your greatest need. It might be suppressed, in large part because whenever your woman leads, it kills your desire to devote to her. But what you will likely discover is that when you don't let her lead, you begin feeling increasingly devoted to her. That is what I discovered for myself when I went through this process. And that is why you need to understand the difference between solution based (leading) communication directing an outcome, and problem based (following) communication not directing an outcome.

When a woman expresses a problem without trying to get any outcome, she is being vulnerable. She is energetically leaving it up to her man to decide what to do. She is not trying to assert herself in any way. There are only four ways a woman can express herself in a way that will inspire your devotion as a man:

1.   Vulnerably expressing her 'need' as the problem.

"I need help." (vulnerable) instead of "I need you to help me." (assertive)

"I need a hug." (vulnerable) instead of "I'd like a hug." (assertive)

"I need space." (vulnerable) instead of "Please leave me alone." (assertive)

When a woman expresses a need vulnerably, she is not trying to get an outcome. She is just sharing herself with her man. It is very vulnerable to share needs in this way.

2.   Vulnerably expressing the problem.

"I can't do this." (vulnerable) instead of "Come help me with this."

"I'm unable to reach the dishes. (vulnerable) instead of "Help me get the dishes."

"I don't have a ride." (vulnerable) instead of "Come pick me up."

When a woman expresses a problem vulnerably, she is not trying to get an outcome. She is communicating that she needs help, which is vulnerable to express.

3. Vulnerably expressing her feeling as the problem.

"I feel frustration."

"I feel sad."

"I feel very anxious right now."

When a woman expresses a feeling vulnerably, she is not trying to get an outcome. She is communicating what is in her heart by exposing it to you, which is extremely vulnerable. The most vulnerable way to share feelings which taps a woman most deeply into her heart is with "I feel" statements.

4. Vulnerably expressing permission to be led

"Can I have some milk?"

"Can I sit with you?"

"Can I have a hug?"

When a woman expresses permission to be led vulnerably, she is not trying to get an outcome. She is communicating that you are fully in charge, and that she respects your role as the leader. She is vulnerably submitting herself to the decision you come up with.

When your woman tries to lead you with offering solutions and trying to get an outcome from you, these are the four ways you must lead her back to expressing herself without outcome. Pay close attention to the difference in how it feels for your woman to express without outcome vs leading you for an outcome. Listen to your body. Trust your body. That is how you will win this game. When your body tells you that you are being led, stop her and lovingly correct her. Do not submit to her leadership.

Don't let her lead!

With this training complete, you are now ready to begin beating each level of the game.

ANTICIPATE HER NEEDS AND WANTS
(LEVEL ONE)

If your woman has a pulse, she has needs and wants. Lots of them. Regardless of whether she is aware of them or not. Regardless of whether she expresses them or not. The absolute best way to stop your woman from leading is to anticipate her needs before she even knows what those needs are. To do this successfully, you must understand your woman well. You must work hard to understand her, by asking questions and observing her. That way you will start to develop a sense and even an intuition of what your woman needs. Both in the short-term and in the long term.

In my marriage I put a lot of attention into what my wife needs so that she doesn't have to ask. We live in a home that we heat with wood in the winter. I know she gets cold easily, whereas I can tolerate cold in my underpants all the way down to near freezing. But I make sure that the fire is lit first thing in the morning, and the heat is above room temperature all day, because I know my wife has a need to feel comfortable and has a narrow temperature range to feel comfortable in,.

When I know my wife is making a meal with potatoes in it I peel them for her, because I know she hates peeling things. I enjoy coming to the rescue and doing it for her.

When my wife is stressed from a long day working, I don't

engage with her at all. I know she needs space to decompress, so I give it to her.

When I am driving with my wife, I am slower around sharp turns or in bad weather than I otherwise would be. I do that because my wife gets easily anxious when she isn't driving, not because I think it is any safer.

When we have been out together for a while without eating, I ask her if she is getting hungry or thirsty so she doesn't need to ask.

When I am talking to my wife and I can sense she is getting sick of talking to me, I get up and leave.

When we are going somewhere I give my wife a specific time that we will leave. I know that she needs to feel secure with specific times so she isn't left guessing.

When we are walking together and we are approaching a door, I take an extra step ahead and open it for her, yes, chivalry is all about anticipating a woman's needs.

I am also focused on anticipating my wife's longer term needs too. I budget our finances to make sure we have lots of savings. I make sure we will have enough for when we have another baby. I make sure we have enough despite any potential unforeseen event. I know that she needs financial security to feel safe.

My goal is to be able to anticipate all of my wife's needs without her having to express them to me. That is how I get a 'perfect score' in this level. That is why I am always thinking ahead of time about what she may need, or even what she may want. I don't meet all of her wants, but I make sure that one way or another, all of her needs are met.

When a man is focused on anticipating his woman's needs, he is automatically fulfilling two of her most important needs: He is making her feel safe, and making her feel cared for. This is very important for a woman to be able to relax and enjoy herself because it allows her to let go of all control in the relationship. Why would she need to control anything when she feels safe and cared for? She can just enjoy the ride.

It's also very easy and fun for a man to anticipate his woman's needs. He has complete freedom to do whatever it takes to put a smile on his woman's face. He isn't being led to do it, he isn't living up to expectations to do it, he's just doing it as a fun gift to take care of his woman. The purpose of the game is to make your woman's smile as big as possible when she sees how well you take care of her, and there is little that is more fun for a man if he loves his woman.

But the game starts to get all screwed up when your woman starts expressing her needs when you already had a handle on meeting them without her saying anything. This is most intolerable when your woman tries to get her needs met by leading towards an outcome by giving solutions.

"Please light the stove."

"Can you light the stove?"

"I want the stove on now."

You must shut this nonsense down immediately. You'll lose the game if you allow her to lead you in this way. Whenever a woman tries to lead like this, just say "No. If you need something, just tell me what the problem is. Do not tell me what to do."

An appropriate thing your woman could say is "I feel cold." That is not leading, and a man will feel good solving this problem for her.

But even if your woman is showing you respect as the leader in this way, it is not good that she said something if you already knew her problem and were planning on solving it for her. The issue is that when she communicates that she needs something, you can no longer give her the gift of anticipating her need and doing it without her saying anything. You can still give her the gift of fulfilling her need. But you can't give her the additional gift of anticipating it and giving it to her without her saying anything.

Sometimes a woman will have to communicate her needs because you are simply not aware of them. But when you do become increasingly aware of certain needs she has and you know what to do to meet them, you must get her to stop communicating anything to get those needs met. The reason she is still communicating those needs to you is because she doesn't fully trust you to meet them. She doesn't realize that you would have anticipated those needs and met them without her even opening her mouth. She probably has a good reason to not trust you because you've been terrible at anticipating her needs in the past. But now you can start doing better.

Unfortunately, if she continues communicating her needs before you anticipate them and meet them, she will continue to lack that trust in you. That will keep her stuck always expressing her needs when she doesn't have to, which takes away from the gift you can give her by anticipating the needs. The only way she will gain that trust is if she says nothing and you still meet her needs. So you must get her to stop communicating those needs completely. Only stop her communicating the needs she has that you know you can meet consistently without her saying anything. You should still encourage her to communicate other needs that you are unaware of and aren't able to anticipate properly.

"Baby I already know you need this. Don't tell me you need this, I've got it taken care of."

This is what I had to do with my wife. She would often tell me that she was cold, when I knew she was cold. Because I had a clear sense of when she was cold, I knew there was no point in her telling me. It was only taking away from the gift I could give her of anticipating her needs. So I told her to stop doing it. I asked her what the minimum temperature was where she starts to feel cold, and she told me. And I told her that my job is to keep the temperature above that, and she doesn't need to tell me anymore. Problem solved.

But this creates another potential problem; stifling her free expression. You don't want to do that. Your woman needs to be able to express herself, and she definitely needs to be able to express her needs when she isn't trying to lead you to meet them. The reason you want her to stop expressing herself in this case is because she doesn't trust you to anticipate her needs. You are breaking the cycle of that lack of trust by getting her to stop communicating and proving to her that you can anticipate her needs. And that will eventually get her to a point where she feels no desire to express that need anymore. That's the goal. Trust building.

If your goal is to build trust, you better take your role of anticipating her needs very seriously. Stick to your word. Do what you said you were going to do. You better be focused on succeeding. If you tell her she doesn't need to tell you anymore, you better be right. Otherwise she will actually start losing trust for you, and you will get even further from your goal. You'll lose this level.

You should set up a fail-safe for when you do drop the ball. Its inevitable that it will happen at some point. You will fail to anticipate a need that you told your woman she did not have to express to you. But you will be ready for that. What you must do is pre-emptively tell your woman that if you fail to properly anticipate her need, you want her to tell you how that made her feel. You need to lead her to tell you that she feels hurt, rejected, disrespected, frustrated, whatever the feeling is. Make her feel safe to tell you by explaining to her that you want her to tell you if you make a mistake. She needs to know that she has a way to communicate to you when she has been waiting for her need to be fulfilled and you aren't taking action. What she feels is information which you need to know. Her being able to share those feelings will reestablish trust when you acknowledge them, and take full responsibility for not doing what you said. Hearing how you negatively emotionally effected your woman will give you the extra motivation to try even harder.

You beat this level when you can anticipate and fulfill many of your woman's needs that can reasonably be anticipated.

You get a perfect score when you are so connected to your woman that you can anticipate all of her needs without her ever saying anything.

DON'T LET HER GIVE YOU STUFF
(LEVEL TWO)

When your woman gives you stuff, she is in the 'giving' role. She is leading to get an outcome of trying to make you happy. Even if she isn't telling you to do anything, she is leading herself to do things for you that you did not ask her to do. Typical gifts that a woman might give you include the following:

Physical gifts: Presents, jewelry, money, trinkets, toys, games, clothes.

Physical touch: Back-rubs, blowjobs, sex, kisses, cuddles.

Acts of service: Packing your bags, cleaning for you, cooking for you.

Words of affirmations: compliments of any kind.

Quality time: calling you on the phone, initiating texts, coming over to see you, initiating conversations, inviting you to do something.

Yes, I covered all the 'love languages'. After seeing some of the things on this list, you might be thinking this is great that your woman anticipates these needs. Or if she isn't anticipating those needs, it would be great if she did. But you need to get her to stop doing all of these things for you, because she is leading. You may be thinking that this is the worst advice that you have ever heard in your entire lifetime. Especially in regards to the blowjobs and sex! But dig deeper.

When your woman gives you things that you *don't* want, she is slowly pushing you away. The more stuff, touch, acts of service, compliments, and time she gives you, the less interested in her you will be. If she really does it to excess, you will begin to feel suffocated. You will lose attraction for her, and you will lose interest in the relationship. And it will be all your fault, because you didn't set a boundary against her giving you things. You let her lead, and you shouldn't have.

When your woman gives you things that you *do* want, she is taking away your ability to lead her to give them to you. You might have wanted that blowjob. You probably did! But how are you going to be the leader in the relationship if your woman initiates by coming over, pulling your pants down, and giving it to you without you telling her you want one? She is putting you in a position where you are the woman! It is the man that is supposed to be in the giving role. He is the one that is supposed to be anticipating his woman's needs and giving her what she wants without asking. The woman is supposed to not anticipate her man's needs at all, and only meet his needs by submitting to his leadership. If you want something from your woman, you can always lead her to give it to you. That's what men do.

The primary underlying reason why a woman gives to her man without asking is that she suffers from self-worth issues. She has been conditioned to believe that her self worth comes from the things she gives, rather than from the person she *is*. What she desperately wants is your reciprocation of love. And she believes that if she only gives enough, she will get it back in return. But she won't get it back, because when a woman gives to a man it actually pushes him away. A man gets pushed away when his woman gives to him because he can sense that she is trying to make up for her low worth. The more she communicates that she has low worth, the less he will be interested in spending time with her. If you allow her to do this with you, you will be allowing her to push you away, which will only make her needier and make her feel like she is worthless.

But self worth is not the only reason men feel pushed away when women give. A woman takes on the giving role and gives to her man without him asking because she thinks that this is what he needs to feel loved. She believes that because it is what *she* needs to feel loved. It is a tragic misapplication of the golden rule. A man doesn't need that to feel loved. A man doesn't need his woman to give him anything, what he needs is for her to receive him fully as a man. A man needs to feel like the 'provider' to feel like a man in the relationship, and being a provider isn't just about making money. It is also about providing love, to his woman's heart. Through his leadership. He feels loved when his woman receives his gifts which he gives her through his leadership. He needs her to submit to those gifts. And show appreciation for those gifts. The magic for a man is in the *giving*, not in the receiving.

A man doesn't need his woman to give him presents. He needs her to light up when he gives her presents.

A man doesn't need his woman to touch him. He needs her to purr with pleasure when he touches her.

A man doesn't need his woman to do a bunch of stuff for him without him asking. He needs her to tell him how happy she is when he does something for her.

A man doesn't need his woman to give him compliments. He needs his woman to tell him how happy she feels because of him giving her a compliment.

A man doesn't need his woman to initiate contact. He needs his woman to be excited and enthusiastic when he contacts her.

But your woman doesn't understand this. She doesn't know what you really need. Because she is seeing the world through her eyes as a woman. She is treating you the way she wants to be treated, and that needs to stop because it's not what you need to feel like a man. It's not what you need to feel devoted to her.

The best thing you can do for her is set a firm expectation:

"Do not give me things unless I tell you I want something. Focus on yourself and what makes *you* happy."

It will be useful for her to understand why you are setting that expectation, because she may be hurt by it. Tell her that you like when she does things for you, but only if you tell her to do them. Tell her that you don't want her anticipating what you need and how you feel, because that prevents her from being in her own body focused on what she needs and how she feels. Tell her that she is important to you and that you want to take care of her.

She will almost certainly not be perfect at adjusting to your expectation. She may feel compelled to give to you. Reassure her that you love her. But do not let her violate your expectation. It will end up hurting her and the relationship if you do. Whenever she tries to give you something without your leadership just kindly tell her:

"Don't do that, love. I didn't say I wanted you to do that."

If you are going to stop your woman from anticipating your needs, you will be putting yourself in a situation where you will have to assert yourself to get your needs met. You do have needs other than to feel received and respected as the leader by your woman. Not many, but some. However you won't be able to rely on your woman any longer to anticipate what you need. You will have to tell her what you need, or what you want. This is very important as a man. This is an opportunity for you to lead. When you lead your woman to meet your needs, you are 'giving' her your leadership.

But this might be difficult for you if you have a belief about not being worthy of having your needs met and don't believe you are intrinsically valuable. Most children were given the message in childhood that their needs didn't matter, and so it will feel very uncomfortable or scary to assert your needs. You may fear judgment, or rejection. Or you may feel guilty or ashamed for asserting your needs because you don't believe you deserve to have them met. But you do deserve them to be met. You must push through whatever discomfort you have and tell your woman what needs you want her to meet.

When I first started to assert my needs with my wife, I realized just how much I had subconsciously been letting fear hold me back. I had no problem asserting needs that were mutually beneficial. For example, it was very easy for me to lead my wife to have sex or to initiate contact with her. Because as much as I enjoy those things, it feels like something I am giving her. My body is a gift to her, and my time is a gift to her. But when it came to needs that were just about me, I found I had more difficulty. Leading her to give me any kind of 'sexual favor' made me feel anxious and also slightly selfish. Even just telling her that I wanted her to make me some cookies was difficult, because it was all about me. I had to push through that.

"Come give me a blowjob."

"Babe, go make me some cookies."

Asserting your needs as a man is direct and clear. It's not controlling, you should not be energetically forcing a woman to meet your needs and desires. Her submission to you should always feel like a choice for her. Ideally it should be enjoyable for her to meet your needs through her submission. A woman will love to submit to her man's needs when her heart is open and she is in a relationship with a strong loving man. But it won't always be something she is thrilled about. She doesn't have to be thrilled about it, but she does have to choose to do it of her own free will because she knows it's what you need or want. It is important that she is willing to meet your needs, assuming that you are willing to meet hers. Meeting needs is what relationships are all about.

I discovered something extraordinary when I stopped letting my wife anticipate my needs. I realized that it feels much better when my wife does something for me through my leadership than when she does it without me asking. When it is through my leadership, I feel like a man. I feel respected. I feel powerful. It feels great that my wife respects my leadership to meet my needs. When my wife does something without me asking it may feel 'nice' at best. But I do not feel like a man in the same way. That is because it's not so much about the 'thing' that I am given. It is about the 'respect' that I am given through her submission. That is what I need as a man. That is also what you need as a man.

This is important to understand because men and women are very different in this respect. A man feels good when his leadership is respected. He enjoys it when his woman does what he says. But a woman feels good when she doesn't have to lead her man to do anything. She enjoys it when her man gives her what she needs without her communicating that she needed it. That is how she feels loved and cared for the most. If she has to lead him to do it, her gut feeling is "does he even want to do this for me, or is he only doing it because I asked him to?"

You beat this level when you usually are able to point out to your woman when she is anticipating your needs and she is receptive to stopping. And also when you are able to get your needs met by telling your woman what you want and she is receptive to meeting them.

You get a perfect score when your woman never anticipates any of your needs and she loves submitting to meet them through your fearless leadership.

DON'T LET HER MOTHER YOU

(LEVEL THREE)

When your woman gives you advice, reminders, and 'pointers', she is in the giving role. She is giving you her leadership. She is doing it because she has a mothering instinct, and you are not acting like a man. You are not being responsible. You aren't telling her that you do not need this from her. She is only trying to help, but by doing so, she is destroying the attraction that you have for her. And she is also losing the attraction that she has for you.

Advice is telling you things that she thinks you should do:

"You would look better in your nice jeans."

"Try washing the dishes with more soap."

"I think you should stop working so hard."

Reminders are questions or statements to remind you of something you should be doing:

"The stove burner is still on."

"You're going to be late for work."

"Did you remember to lock the door?"

Pointers are statements to bring your attention to something she wants you to be aware of:

"The sink is disgusting."

"The lawn isn't cut."

"There is a stop sign ahead."

When a woman mothers, it may seem so innocent. It seems like it is not a big deal. But it is actually a huge deal. What she is communicating is that she doesn't trust you to be responsible. If she trusted you, she would have no reason to give you advice, reminders, or pointers. If she can't fully trust you, it means that she cannot fully submit to you. For her to be able to fully submit, she needs to fully feel safe. And a man who is irresponsible is not safe.

That should be reason enough to become more responsible. If you cannot find the motivation for yourself, then do it for her. Do it because she needs to feel completely safe and trust you completely. You want to fulfill that need for her, because you are devoted to her. You have the power to make her feel completely free to let go with you and not worry about anything. You can give her an incredible experience where she can relax and enjoy herself because she fully knows that her man has got a handle on things.

You probably do forget to turn the burner off. You probably do forget appointments. You probably do irresponsible things that are not the best decisions. These are things that you should work on. You need to be willing to turn yourself into a self-improvement machine to make your woman feel amazing. Your goal is to become so responsible that your woman can completely relax around you. Reflect carefully on all the ways that you are not being fully responsible in your life.

Are you always true to your word?

Do you always remember everything you were meant to remember?

Do you always show up for things on time?

Are you considerate of your woman's feelings?

Do you fulfill the expectations you set for yourself and committed to around the house?

Is your safety, your woman's safety, and (if applicable) your children's safety a top priority?

Do you clearly communicate with your woman so she knows what is expected of her and what you will be doing?

If you answered 'no' to any of these questions, you have work to do. You have to work on becoming the most responsible man you can be for your woman so that she feels completely safe with you. That is one of her most important needs. But you can only fulfill that need when your personal growth comes from your own leadership. If you fulfill the need by submitting to her mothering, you are not leading. You are not being her man. You are being her good little boy.

Being your woman's good little boy by submitting to her leadership is problematic because you will never enjoy doing it. You will very quickly lose all motivation to develop yourself and become the man your woman needs when she is mothering you. If anything, you will feel motivated to do the opposite. You will feel compelled to resist and not budge from being the way you are. That resistance is a good thing. It is your instincts telling you that it is wrong to submit to your woman. You should listen to your instincts. It is wrong because you are disrespecting yourself as a man.

But even if you did end up submitting to your woman's leadership, you won't make her feel safe. You won't make her feel relaxed. And you definitely won't make her feel attracted to you. It doesn't matter how responsible you end up becoming by being true to your word and remembering everything and showing up for things on time. Because you are being irresponsible by submitting to your woman's leadership. You are being irresponsible by not setting boundaries against her leading you. You are being irresponsible by not leading her to do what you want her to do. You are being irresponsible by not telling her the truth about how her leading you is inappropriate and is pushing you away from her.

And if you are being irresponsible, your woman won't feel safe.

That is why the first thing you must do is tell your woman to stop mothering you, and then lead her to express how she feels instead. You do not need a mother. You need a lover.

"Babe, if I need your advice I will ask for it. Stop giving it to me without me asking, thankyou."

"Stop giving me reminders."

"I can sense that you are telling me this so that I will do something about it. Stop that, you're leading."

This is not meant to hurt her. It might hurt her, but this should not be your intention. Your intention should be to make it clear what behavior is unacceptable to you, and any form of leadership from her should not be acceptable. These can't just be empty words. You must commit yourself to making this into a firm boundary. A line in the sand. One which you defend whenever necessary. Don't let her get away with mothering. You must let her know when she does it, and make it clear that she should not be doing it. There is no need to be mean about it. You shouldn't be mean. You should be loving. Loving, but firm.

Once you set this boundary, a woman may have trouble complying. She may have feelings of anxiety or irritation that are compelling her to mother you. When you tell her to stop mothering you, those feelings will not go away. It can be painful for her to hold on to those feelings. She needs an outlet. And you can give her one, with your devoted leadership. Tell her that if she feels anything because of your behavior, that she should tell you how she feels vulnerably. With "I feel" statements. Be willing to ask her why she feels that way after she expresses her feeling.

"I feel embarrassment"…"Because I care about what people will think of me when we go out and you wear sweatpants. "

"I feel anxious."… "Because I start thinking about the house burning down whenever the burner is left on."

"I feel irritation."…"Because the sink is still messy and you said you'd clean it."

When a woman expresses vulnerably, she isn't leading to get an outcome, she is only expressing. Now you are able to take her seriously without submitting to her leadership. Her feelings are important, and it's important that she feels good around you. You can now hear what she has to say, and choose to adjust your behavior as a gift to her, because you love making her feel good. You can do this through your leadership, because she is no longer trying to change you through her leadership.

I now dress nicer when I go out with my wife. I used to dress like a complete slob when I was out with her. One step up from a homeless person. I did that because I could not possibly care less what people think of how I dress. My identity is in no way effected by what people think of how I look, and so it seems like a waste of time to dress nicely. However, I do care very much about how my wife feels. I do not want her to feel embarrassed around me, I want her to feel sexy around me, and lucky to be with me. Once I led her to stop giving me advice and asked her how she felt, I understood I was hurting her by dressing poorly. I wanted to make her feel good, so I started dressing better when we went out. Through my leadership.

My wife's vulnerable expression helped me become more responsible. I don't care much about how other people think or feel about me. But I do care about how I make other people feel, especially my wife. By her being vulnerable with her feelings, it gave me the opportunity to reflect on how my behavior effects her emotionally. I chose to be more responsible for my behaviors as a gift to her, because I want to make her feel as good as possible. But only when its through my leadership.

I now work very hard to remember things. I have a terrible memory because my mind is always focused on the big picture. I'm thinking about the next chapter of my book when I am cooking bacon and eggs. This lack of focus on the mundane in front of me results in me forgetting to do a lot of things. Like remembering to turn off the stove burner after my bacon and eggs are done. I know I should remember these things, but it is very difficult. However, I do care about how my wife feels. I do not want her to feel anxious about the house burning down, I want her to be able to relax and enjoy herself. Once I led her to stop giving me reminders and asked her how she felt, I understood that I was hurting her by having a bad memory. I wanted to make her feel relaxed, so I started working harder to remember things. Through my leadership.

Once again, my wife's vulnerable expression helped me become more responsible. I am not worried about the house burning down (it's an electric stove). But I do care about my wife's anxiety. By her being vulnerable with her feelings, I realized the negative effect I was having on her. And that negative effect is much more than just the anxiety about the stove. A man who can't remember things is not trustworthy and a woman will have a difficult time relaxing and submitting to a man she cannot trust. I chose to be more responsible and remember things because I want her to feel completely safe with me. I want her to be able to trust me completely.

I now work very hard to clean the sink. It is something that I chose as a responsibility in the household. It is the only thing I clean, and I do it to make my wife's life a little easier. My natural tendency is to let the dishes pile up until we are out of dishes, and then do all of them when I have no choice. Or just buy new dishes and throw the old dirty ones in the garbage. I just don't care about dishes. But I do care about how my wife feels. I do not want her to feel irritated or frustrated or disrespected. And she feels irritated and sometimes disrespected when I let those dishes pile up, and her tendency is to give out pointers about what she sees. Once I led her to stop giving me pointers and asked her how she felt, I understood the stress that I was causing her. It was difficult for me to understand because a dirty sink or a dirty house doesn't cause me any stress whatsoever, but her being vulnerable helped me understand. I then started working hard to keep the sink clean. Through my leadership.

Once again, my wife's vulnerable expression helped me become more responsible. I do not care about a dirty sink. But I do care about my wife feeling irritated. I also do not want her to lose trust in me when I say I am going to do something. By her being vulnerable with her feelings, I understood how important it was to be responsible when I say I am going to do something. A man who is not true to his word, even with insignificant little things, is not trustworthy and he is communicating disrespect to his woman. I chose to be more responsible and be true to my word because I want her to feel respected and trust me.

Once you shift your woman away from mothering you and towards expressing her feelings, you will notice a big shift in your desire to become a better man for your woman. Instead of trying to change to get her to stop annoying you with her mothering, you will feel compelled to change because it makes you feel good to make her feel good.

You beat this level when you usually tell your woman when she is mothering you and she is receptive to stopping and expressing how she feels.

You get a perfect score when your woman never mothers you and only expresses her feelings.

DON'T LET HER SET EXPECTATIONS

(LEVEL FOUR)

You as the man are responsible for making all of the expectations in the relationship. You decide the chores. You decide what behavior constitutes cheating. You decide how you both treat each other. You decide how your woman talks to you. You decide how problems are dealt with. You decide how children are raised. You decide on how money is spent and saved. You decide everything. And you need to make sure that your woman doesn't try to decide anything.

When a woman has expectations and expresses those expectations in a relationship, she is leading. She is trying to set her expectations as ones that you are to live up to. She wants you to submit to her expectations. You must put a stop to this. A woman should not get to have expectations in a relationship. The relationship must be based on the man's inner vision. *Your* inner vision.

When a woman is unable to let go of her expectations in a relationship, the result is that she will try negotiating to create a compromise between your expectations and hers. This is the trap that many couples get into. The woman says what she wants. The man says what he wants. And then they make a final joint decision together. This is co-leading. It can happen with chores. It can happen with finances. It can happen with deciding how children will be raised. It can happen with 'rules' of the relationship such as what constitutes cheating. And worse, when partners can't agree on fair expectations, they start debating.

Any kind of negotiating in a relationship sets a dynamic based on competition. You are trying to get your needs met, and she is trying to get her needs met. And you are competing against each other to get those needs met. She is trying to make you change your inner vision of your relationship, and add parts of her inner vision into it instead. You are dividing up a pie and each of you is trying to get a bigger slice. Even if you are respectfully 'collaborating' together, there is still an element of competition involved. There is still a mindset where each partner is on their own, trying to get a 'compromise' that is beneficial to them and less beneficial to their partner.

This is a big problem because a man doesn't want to compromise. He is not programmed to compromise. He is not programmed to water down his inner vision to make room for his woman's inner vision. He is programmed to devote to his woman through his leadership. As soon as he gets into the mindset of competing, he will want to do what all men do when they compete; he will try to win. He will win by getting the bigger piece of the pie. He will want to resist as much as he can to avoid changing his inner vision. And to make matters worse, he will then have a very hard time keeping his agreements, because nothing he does will be through his leadership. If it's not through his leadership, it's not fun, and it's then hard to be responsible for what he says he will do.

This is also a big problem because a woman doesn't want to compromise either. She is not programmed to do so, even if she thinks she is. She is programmed to be cared for through her man's leadership. She is programmed to submit to her man's inner vision. As soon as she gets into the mindset of competing, she can no longer relax. She has to stay on guard and assert herself to get her needs met through the compromised expectations. She will become stressed because she is taking on the responsibility of making sure that things happen. That is why not letting your woman lead isn't just for your benefit, it is also for hers.

When my wife and I used to negotiate expectations, I had a very hard time taking them seriously. When my negotiated expectation was to sometimes do the laundry, it took all of my willpower to actually do it when I was supposed to. I hate cleaning things. That changed when I stopped letting my wife negotiate. Once I made all of the decisions for both of us I began to feel responsible for honoring them. I don't do laundry anymore, but I do clean dishes. I do take out garbage. I do fix things. I do go get groceries. And I do it all for my wife. These are my expectations that I made, they were not negotiated. I now take these tasks far more seriously. I feel like a man because I am in charge, and it makes my wife feel like a woman because she can relax knowing I've got my side of things taken care of.

The best way to avoid a dynamic where your woman isn't trying to make any expectations is to proactively tell your woman what your expectations are. Assume leadership and tell her the way you want things to be. When you are very clear in your expectations from the start, you are leading. And it leaves much less room for your woman to try leading by adding in her own expectations. If you passively wait and stay silent about your expectations, your woman is going to come up with all of her own to fill the void. You are doing her a disservice by not being clear from the start. You are making her feel unsafe and stressed because she is unclear of how things are. You force her into a position of adding in her own expectations to feel safe.

Think about what you want your relationship to look like. Envision how your 'perfect' relationship would operate. What expectations would be needed to create this perfect relationship? These should be expectations that are based on what is best for the relationship. This means it should be expectations that are fair and consider your woman's needs. If you both work full time, is it a good expectation that she does all the cleaning and cooking and takes care of the kids? If you are both doing your equal share, is it a good expectation that you get to spend way more money than she does on things you want but don't benefit her? If she feels easily insecure, is it a good expectation that you can go out all night to a party and not communicate with her the entire time? Will that be good for the relationship if she is overworked, resentful, and insecure? Probably not.

Do not make any assumptions about whether your woman agrees with your unsaid expectations. You must make them clear. If you don't, it will lead to a lot more conflict and problems later. Assume she doesn't know your expectations unless you tell her what they are. Treat your relationship like you would if you were managing a business. Do you assume that your employees know your expectations? If not, you shouldn't assume your woman knows your expectations either. Assuming that your woman knows your expectations is very weak leadership.

When my wife and I moved to our new house, she didn't have a job and I had given up my local business and wasn't working either. I told her that I wanted her to cook and clean, and I would be working outside making our property self-sufficient. But things changed months later when my wife found a 9-5 job and I stopped working outside and started my relationship coaching business. My expectations had to change too. It would have been unfair to have her do everything inside the home, even though I was working longer hours. It would have been irresponsible of me to not adjust my expectations based on the new circumstances. That was why I told her I would do the dishes for her, and cook her breakfast.

I did not state my opinion about what we should do. I stated my expectation about what we *will* do. I was clear, direct, and firm. I assumed leadership. I knew it was my place to lead my own expectations. I knew what I wanted and I knew it was the right expectation to have. If you are stating opinions, you are opening up the dynamic for your woman to lead by negotiating. You don't want that. I know I certainly didn't want that. That's why I was firm. I did not want my wife to lead.

"I would like you to cook meals and take care of the children while I work."

"I want us to tell each other everything. No lying or withholding the truth."

"I want us to be exclusive, and that means no flirting or 'emotional' cheating."

And the most important expectation of all which is very relevant to this book:

"Don't lead me. If I do or say or expect something that hurts you in any way or makes you feel something negative, just tell me how you feel."

Which leads me to my next point: Your woman may disagree with you about what is fair or acceptable, and she may start trying to argue her opinions. She may say:

"It's not fair that I have to do all the cleaning."

or

"You are trying to control me!"

You cannot tolerate that. You cannot allow her to debate you on your expectations and try to negotiate with you. She is disrespecting your leadership by doing this. You must lead her to be vulnerable.

You can say something like:

"I don't care what your expectations are. I care about how you feel. How do you feel right now that I have asked you to do all of the cleaning?"

Your goal is to get your woman to vulnerably express her feelings without trying to get an outcome. Get her to make "I feel" statements, and then lead her to explain why she feels that way. You must make it clear that you are not interested in living up to her expectations, you are only interested in how she feels, because you deeply care about how she feels. You must help your woman let go of her expectations and instead learn to express herself vulnerably. She needs to learn to express how your expectations and leadership make her feel. You need to be able to lead her to do that, and then adjust your leadership as necessary so that she is happy. It should be your expectation that your woman expresses how she feels instead of negotiating her expectations.

This is the most important expectation you can set for your woman. It is communicating two very important expectations at the same time: It is saying that you are in charge as the leader, not your woman. And it is saying that you will hold space for your woman's feelings because they are important to you. You must make this abundantly clear to your woman. You must make her understand that you expect her to be very honest with how she feels with you. You must lead her every chance you get for her to vulnerably express her feelings. This isn't just important for her so that she has a voice. It is also important for you, so that you understand how your leadership is impacting your woman, giving you the information you need to adjust when necessary.

It is very important that your woman is free to express how she feels. As a devoted man, your job is to incorporate how your woman feels into your inner-vision. Your inner-vision is yours and yours alone, with your own expectations. But the center of your inner vision should include a happy woman. A woman who feels happy, respected, loved, safe, appreciated, and cared for. So while you should not care that your woman has an expectation that you do half of the chores, you definitely should care that your woman feels disrespected if you lead her to do all of the chores.

This is how I determine all of my expectations with my wife, and that shows when it comes to how we manage our finances. My ideal relationship would be that I am fully in charge of all finances and bank accounts, she hands over her pay-cheque to me, and I give her a monthly allowance for spending money for her own stuff. That way she wouldn't have to worry about any kind of budgeting and could just enjoy spending on whatever she wants for herself based on what our household can afford. I am an excellent financial planner, and I make very good decisions with money for our household. Which will benefit her long-term happiness.

However, my wife has a deep seated fear of not having control. I am continuing to lead her deeper into letting go of control at her own pace. But I do not believe in forcing her to do anything she isn't ready for. I do not want her to feel unnecessary anxiety. And I definitely do not want her to feel resentment towards me. So I adjusted my expectations with our finances, because I care deeply about how she feels. Instead, I led her to contribute a sizable portion of her paycheck to me each month so I can better manage the household. Another sizable portion she keeps for our savings. And my expectation is that she doesn't spend a large amount of money when it is better used for the future. She submits to that expectation.

I love adjusting my expectations for my wife to make her feel happy, safe, and loved. My inner-vision has some flexibility, because I am devoted to her heart. But I only enjoy adjusting my expectations when my wife respects me enough to vulnerably express how she feels, and doesn't try to negotiate or control those expectations. When she tries negotiating, I lose any interest in devoting to her. I will resist all of her attempts at trying to lead me and pushing her expectations onto me. I am not open for negotiating, and you as a man shouldn't be either with your woman.

You beat this level when all of the expectations in the relationship are yours and your woman is working towards meeting them.

You get a perfect score when your woman meets all of your expectations in your perfect inner-vision, without resistance.

DON'T LET HER DIRECT YOU
(LEVEL FIVE)

A woman will have lots of needs and wants in a relationship, and many of those you will not be able to anticipate. No matter how good you get at anticipating her needs and wants, sometimes she will have to express to you that she needs something

You are probably stronger than your woman. Taller than her. And more capable at 'doing' a lot of things than her. Women tend to be more emotionally gifted, and men tend to be more gifted in accomplishing 'tasks'. To complicate things further, a woman tends to be tasked with taking care of the inside of a home and taking care of the children while a man works at a job and out in the yard. Even if a woman also works, that is the typical dynamic, and it is instinctually driven. Men provide, women nurture. It is natural, but it also results in a woman requiring a lot of help at home when her man is in the home with her. She will be communicating that she needs your help opening things, fixing things, carrying things, reaching things, understanding things, and purchasing things.

Which is great. A devoted man loves doing things for his woman. A man's greatest need is to give to his woman. That is what fulfills him. There is nothing better for a man than giving to his woman and making her feel happy, safe, and loved. But the giving must come from his leadership for it to be enjoyable. If it comes from his submission to her leadership, he will not enjoy it. He will hate it. And typically when a woman communicates that she needs something, she does it by directing her man towards an outcome. She is leading you. She is the one in control, and you are submitting to her leadership. She isn't doing it to emasculate you, but you need to teach her a better way. That's your job.

Here are the most common ways a woman will try to direct a man:

"Can you open this pickle jar?" (Asked as a directive.)

"Open this pickle jar for me please." (Stated as a directive.)

"I need you to open this pickle jar." (Stated as a directive.)

"I want / I'd like you to open this pickle jar. (Stated as a directive.)

If you are unsure if your woman is being directive, listen to what your body tells you. When she is directing you in any way, you will not feel good. You will feel something resembling slight annoyance or irritation. Listen to that feeling, it is telling you the truth; your woman is trying to lead. That feeling is telling you that something is wrong, and that you need to fix it. You can fix it by telling her "no". And then leading her to communicate without trying to get an outcome in one of these ways:

"Can I have some help opening this pickle jar?" (Asked permissively without outcome.)

"I'm unable to open this pickle jar." (Stated problem without outcome.)

"I need help opening this pickle jar." (Stated need without outcome.)

"I feel frustration trying to open this pickle jar." (Stated vulnerable feeling without outcome.)

Ok the last one would be very weird in this situation. But in other contexts it would be appropriate.

You must actually teach her this form of communication, and you must teach her why it is so important to you. Luckily you can teach her both lessons, because all of the information you need is in this book. Tell her that you are in charge, and you don't want her to lead. Tell her she doesn't need to lead you, because you love taking care of her. Tell her she only needs to express her problem or express permission for a solution, and you will usually be happy to give her what she needs or wants.

When a woman communicates without trying to get an outcome, it should feel good in your body. You should feel compelled to want to help, because she is not placing a burden on you with her leadership. She is not trying to change your inner-vision. That is why it is so important that you lead your woman to express without trying to get an outcome. Her needs matter, but you will only feel compelled to meet her needs if she isn't trying to get you to meet them. She will not understand why you are disinterested in meeting her needs if you are resistant and irritable. She will think it is because you do not care about her and her needs. When really it is because you do not want to be led, and cannot enjoy doing things for her if it is through your submission. You are setting an expectation for how she talks to you as a gift for her. So that you will feel joy in meeting her needs which will make her happy.

By telling her 'no' you are also helping her learn to trust you and to believe that she is worthy of her needs being met without her trying to assert herself. A woman asserts herself to meet her needs because deep down she believes that she is not worthy of having her needs met just by expressing them. She believes you will not care to meet them unless she asserts herself. You are helping her learn that she means so much to you that you will meet her needs without her putting in any effort to get them met. But she can't learn that until you stop letting her lead, and lead her towards expressing her needs without trying to get an outcome. Lead her towards expressing that way, and make her feel comfortable and safe to express that way.

"No, But I'll do it if you nicely ask me permission."

I've said that to my wife before. It felt awkward at first. Much of what I tell men to do here will feel awkward. You will be reclaiming your role as a man, and that feels uncomfortable. It may feel like you are disrespecting your woman by talking to her like she is beneath you. But you are disrespecting her by leading her with love, and devoting to her heart. If you talked to her with condescending energy then you'd be talking to her like she is beneath you. But if you lovingly teach and correct her, and you lovingly adjust your leadership based on how your woman feels, then you are treating her like an equal. That is how a man gives his love to his woman. Ignore what you are feeling and push on.

If you remain weak and do not learn to say 'no' to her leadership, you will grow to resent her. You will not enjoy meeting her needs, and you will allow her to push you away with her leadership. She will not understand what is happening. The relationship will die because you don't know how to give her the loving gift of telling her 'no' and leading her to communicate to you without trying to get an outcome.

This was one of the major turning points for me in my marriage. My wife is very direct and assertive with getting her needs met. But her assertiveness made me not want to meet any of her needs, because I do not enjoy being led. I did not even realize that what I was resisting the entire time was being led, rather than resisting meeting her needs. But I had no idea for years what to do about it. Usually I would just say "no" when it was something big that I didn't want to do. And that would result in my wife resenting me a little bit more each time because I was communicating that I didn't care about her. I would say 'yes' when it was something small that made sense to help her with, even though it didn't feel good to do it. And that would result in me feeling further pushed away and disconnected from her.

Allowing this dynamic to continue results in very hyper-independent relationships. Your woman will slowly learn to not rely on you to take care of her. She will be forced to harden herself. She will toughen up and start doing things increasingly for herself. She will start to believe that she cannot rely on you for much, and can only rely on herself. This is not a good thing. The healthiest relationships are ones where both partners are heavily reliant on each other. Not in an addictive codependent way, but instead in an *inter*dependent way. Humans thrive in interdependent relationships.

A codependent relationship is one where your woman is reliant on you for everything and she brings nothing to the table. She needs you for help all the time and is needy, always requiring your energy. She feels like a constant burden that needs to be taken care of to be able to function. She is a taker, and that will quickly wear on a man. It will drain his energy because he feels needed but isn't getting anything back. His woman is an energy black hole. She can never stay happy for long. She always needs something from him. She needs him to save her. In these relationships, the man feels like a parent, because his woman was never parented properly in childhood.

But an independent relationship isn't significantly better. I used to think it was the gold standard for relationships, and I was always focused on working towards becoming increasingly independent and not 'needing' anything from my relationship. But this is ultimately unfulfilling because a man needs to feel needed. He needs to feel like there is a purpose to him being in the relationship. He needs to feel like his woman needs his gifts of time, energy, money, affection, service, love. If he doesn't feel his woman needs him, then he gets bored and feels like he doesn't have a role with his woman.

The real gold comes from an interdependent relationship. This is where a man gives to his woman. He takes care of her by doing things for her and meeting her needs. But he gets back so much. He gets back respect which makes him feel like a man. He gets back positive energy which energizes him and makes him want to do more for her. He gets back her submission so that his own needs and wants are met. He gets back love which makes him want to work his hardest for her. Instead of his energy getting sucked into a black hole, it becomes multiplied and returned to him.

But a sustainable interdependent relationship is only possible when a man is giving to his woman through his leadership. When he feels respected as the leader, the giving is energizing, especially when his woman is appreciative of his effort. When he doesn't feel respected as the leader, the giving is draining, even if his woman is appreciative of his effort. The giving must come through his leadership or not at all.

I created a sustainable interdependent relationship in my marriage by learning how to set boundaries against my wife directing me to meet her needs and wants. By leading her to communicate without trying to get an outcome, it has made me feel a deep desire to care for her and meet all of her needs, and many of her wants.

When she says "Can I have some coffee." I get her some coffee.

When she says "I can't reach these plates." I take the plates down for her.

When she says "I feel irritation (about a mess)." I clean up the mess.

When she says "I need some alone time." I give her alone time.

I love meeting her needs and wants, but only when it is through my leadership.

However, by being the leader, that also means you reserve the right to say 'no' to anything your woman wants. Sometimes giving her what she wants, even through your leadership, will end up hurting the relationship over all. You need to be willing to draw the line by understanding the bigger picture and how you saying 'yes' may negatively effect what you can give your woman in the future. It is OK to say 'no' sometimes. It is necessary to do so.

When she says "Can I have a 50,000$ car?" I don't give her a 50,000$ car.

My wife hasn't asked for this, but if she did, I would say 'no'. It isn't in our budget right now, and fulfilling her want when there are better things we could spend that money on, or invest than money in, would be irresponsible. Especially because we have a much cheaper brand new car!

It is optional to meet your woman's wants, but it should not be optional to meet her needs. It is important that you know how to distinguish the difference between the two. Wants are a nice bonus. They are icing on the cake. They make your woman happier. But they are not necessary for her to thrive. Whereas needs are the cake. If they go unmet, your woman will become less radiant. She will become resentful, hurt, and guarded.

It might make your woman happy for all of her wants to be fulfilled. It might make you happy to see your woman happy. But it is the wrong decision. You need to be able to base your leadership choices on the best interest of the relationship short-term and long-term. If you base your choices on the short-term happiness of your woman, you are not being a good leader. The same is true if her wants takes away from what you need to be doing in your job or business to the point where it hurts the relationship. If it takes away from what you need to do to recharge yourself, you shouldn't do it. If fulfilling your woman's wants interfere with your needs or your woman's needs, you shouldn't do it.

My wife needs a car, because she needs to be able to travel. But she doesn't need a 50,000$ car, that's a want.

My wife needs quality time with me, because she needs to be able to connect. But she doesn't need three hours to spend with me a day, that's a want.

My wife needs to be able to express her feelings with me, because she has a need to feel heard. But she doesn't need to be talking to me about things I don't care about and drain me, that's a want.

My wife needs to have a comfy house to live in, because she needs to feel at home. But she doesn't need me to make her various wood pieces to decorate the home, that's a want.

My wife needs me to fulfill some of her wants, because she needs to feel loved and appreciated. But she doesn't need me to fulfill all of her wants, that would be impossible!

Your woman also needs to be OK with you saying 'no' to some of her wants. If she isn't OK with it, then it means she had an expectation of you to give to her. If she has expectations that means she feels entitled to your time, energy, and love. That is not OK You need to explain to her why that isn't OK She is not entitled to your time, energy, and love. Once entitlement gets in the way, it is no longer enjoyable for you to give. If you are going to lead, she needs to be OK with your 'no'. Otherwise she isn't really trusting and respecting you to lead. It's just an act.

You beat this level when you usually point out when your woman is directing you and she is receptive to working on expressing without trying to get an outcome to get her needs and wants met.

You get a perfect score when your woman never directs you to get her needs or wants met.

DON'T LET HER MANIPULATE
(LEVEL SIX)

Manipulation is leadership done by stealth. When a woman manipulates, she is trying to get an outcome without you realizing that she is trying to get one. She is trying to be the leader while pretending you are leading and deciding. This doesn't have to be conscious, and it often is not conscious. There are many different ways that a woman may try manipulating an outcome:

1. Hinting about what she wants to try to get her man to give it to her: "Hey that necklace looks so nice."

When a woman hints, she rarely realizes that she is manipulating. She is trying to get her man to lead to meet her needs, without her asserting herself. But the very act of hinting is actually leading, because she is trying to get an outcome. It's worse than just directly leading and saying "I want that necklace." because it leaves men confused and simultaneously feeling like they are being led via manipulation.

That is why a man will often tell a woman to just be direct, but this is bad advice. This advice results in women acting more like men by asserting their needs. Men might think they want that, but they quickly find they hate that too. Women intuitively know this, and that is part of the reason they will often try to get their needs met with hinting. They know it doesn't feel good to directly lead a man, and they know a man doesn't respond well to it.

The third option is to communicate without trying to get an outcome. The best thing a woman could do in most cases where she is hinting is permissively ask for what she wants.

"Can I have that necklace?"

When it comes from a permissive place, a man will feel like a leader, because the decision is fully put on him. This is contrary to "Can you buy me that necklace?" where there is subtle directive leading to outcome. It is directive because it is made to be about him, rather than about her. You as the man need to make your woman aware of her attempts at manipulating through hinting, and lead her to ask you permissively when she wants something.

"Don't hint at what you want. If you want something from me, ask me permission for it."

2. Withholding something to get something else from a man. "I'm still not in the mood for sex because you haven't taken me out."

When a woman withholds something for an exchange, she is communicating disrespect for her man. This is coming from a place of deep insecurity because she doesn't think her needs will be met without manipulation. She is just trying to get her needs met in the best way she knows how. She is playing out her childhood traumas. The worst thing you could do is emotionally punish her for that by getting angry, when all she was trying to do was get what she needs. Don't punish, lead her. Make her aware of what she is doing, and tell her how she can do it better.

When you lead a woman away from manipulating in this way, it needs to be firm. But you are really doing it for her. She is hurting herself by trying to manipulate in this way. Even if she ends up getting what she wants from you, she will never be satisfied. A woman cannot be satisfied with getting her needs met by manipulating a man to meet them. A man isn't giving to her out of love when he caves to her manipulation, and she knows it's not love. Yet what she craves most is to get love. That is why you must stop her manipulating and give her what she needs of your own free will when she stops trying to manipulate you into it.

"I am not going to take you out to get sex from you. You are being manipulative and you need to stop that. If you are hurt about me not taking you out, tell me how you feel. What I care about is your feelings."

3. Lying to stop her man from doing something. "I didn't talk to that guy."

A woman is dishonest because she fears the consequences of her honesty. She fears judgment, abandonment, rejection, or her needs not being met in the future. Many women (like men) have been conditioned to lie to avoid bad consequences in child-hood, and this will carry on in her relationships. And the more out of integrity a woman's behavior is, the more she will have to lie to cover it up. This is leading because she is trying to get an outcome that avoids a consequence.

An extension of lying is truth omission. Truth omission is when there is something that should be said, that you would want to know about. She knows that you would want to know, but she omits the truth by avoiding talking about it. She may not technically tell a lie. But she is hiding the truth by manipulating conversation to avoid it.

You need to make a firm boundary against lying and truth omission. It is completely unacceptable and will destroy your relationship. This needs to be a very clear expectation, and you need to communicate that you will quickly lose trust in your woman if she lies to you. The bigger the lie or omission, the bigger the loss of trust.

"This is a relationship based on honesty, I do not want either of us to lie to each other, ever. I do not want us to hide the truth from each other, ever. If you don't tell me the truth, I won't be able to trust you."

But to prevent your woman from lying, you need to role-model truth telling. You need to become 100% honest about everything. You need to tell her what you think about her and her behavior, even if it hurts her. You need to tell her about anything you are hiding from her or want to hide from her, even if it hurts her. Even if it risks destroying the relationship or her respect for you, you need to do it. You need to set this level of honesty as one of your principles with how you lead a relationship. If you can't lead honestly, then you can't expect your woman to be honest either.

You also need to be able to provide a safe space for your woman's honesty. The reason that women learn to lie in the first place was they were taught by their parents that being honest has consequences. They would fess up to something bad they did or thought, and they would be judged or punished for that honesty. This is tricky, because when a woman does something unacceptable, like flirting with a man, and she is honest about it, that can be hard to not be upset about. It's not the honesty that is the problem, it's the behavior she was honest about. But what matters is how you react to the honesty about her behavior.

Learn to become completely non-judgmental and accepting of whatever she tells you. Don't react. Let her know that you appreciate her honesty and that you can trust her more because of it. You can and also should address the problem behavior she is admitting to if it needs to be addressed. Be able to forgive her for it as long as she is taking accountability for it and is committed to working on it. If she does something that permanently breaks trust with you, such as cheating, you may have to let her go. Though even with cheating, it can sometimes be forgiven without becoming a doormat for repeat behavior, depending on the circumstances.

"Thank-you for being honest. I know that must have been very difficult."

4. Leading questions to try to get a man to do something. "Are you going to wear your nice clothes?"

Leading questions are questions that are not asked purely out of curiosity. There is a hidden intent to lead a man to do something by jogging his memory or making him realize it is a good idea. This one can be very subtle. If you sense that your woman is asking questions for this reason, a good answer is just to say you aren't going to do it. When she asks why, tell her you sense that she was trying to get you to do it, so now you don't want to do it. A follow-up more in-depth explanation may be required.

5. Giving gifts of time, energy, love, acts of service etc to get reciprocation. "I bought you something."

Giving to get is a very common strategy that women use to manipulate a man. She has a belief that she is not worthy enough to get a man's gifts unless she gives to him, and so she will give to him in the hopes that he reciprocates. That is a big reason why a woman who anticipates a man's needs is often very off-putting. There is usually an intent to get reciprocation underneath the giving, one that she may not even be aware of. To deal with it, follow the advice in that chapter. Get her to stop giving. If you sense it was done to try to get reciprocation, you can tell her that too. Always be honest by directly telling your woman about any behaviors that are inappropriate.

"I can sense that you are giving to me to try to get something back. Stop doing that. If I didn't ask you for something, don't give it to me."

6. Perception management to get a man to see you a certain way. "I made you cookies."

A woman will often manipulate to get her man to see her a certain way based on her identity. If she identifies with being kind, she might do nice things so he sees her as kind. If she identifies with being strong, she might create a tough appearance of strength and not let him in. If she identifies with being successful, she might brag about her accomplishments. If she identifies with being smart, she might show off her intelligence by teaching him things. You get the idea.

When a woman does this to a man, she is using him to validate herself. She is leading him to perceive her a certain way, and ideally react to her in a certain way. This is done because she has difficulty validating herself, and needs someone external to her to feel good about herself. Everybody wants validation for their identity, and there is absolutely nothing wrong with that desire. But there is a big difference between your woman wanting to be validated for her identity, and her trying to manipulate you into validating it. The best way to deal with this is to respectfully call her out on her behavior, and get her to express the underlying feelings, which is usually some form of insecurity.

"You are trying to get my approval. Stop that. Are you feeling insecure right now?"

Get her to discuss her feelings and then reassure her. It is perfectly fine for a woman to feel insecure and needy for approval. But she needs to own it. She needs to express how she actually feels rather than trying to manipulate you into giving her love. This will make you feel compelled to give her love. Because now she isn't trying to control you into giving it to her.

7. Vulnerably stating problems (which is what this book is helping men lead their woman to do). But she does it for the purpose of trying to get an outcome. "I don't know how to do this." / "I feel sad." / "Can I have some coffee?"

That's right! Everything can be used for manipulation. There is nothing that your woman can say that is exempt from potentially being used to manipulate. And when you do lead your woman to stop leading you, you may notice that even though the words are right, something feels 'off'. Your woman is trying to get an outcome. This isn't done on purpose, it is very hard to fully let go of control all of the time and just express, trusting that her man will take care of her. If a woman has difficulty letting go of control when she starts expressing problems instead of solutions, she will continue to lead, but do so covertly.

I noticed that my wife started manipulating outcomes after I started leading her to communicate problems without trying to get outcomes. The irony is that my wife is a very direct woman, she used to just tell everything to me straight, including telling me when she wanted something. She would lead me, directly. That always turned me off and made me lose interest in devoting to her, but I didn't know what to do about it. Until I learned to lead her to express problems instead of solutions. What I noticed was that sometimes her expression would be pure and I'd feel compelled to jump up to help her. Other times it felt off and I had no desire to help. When it felt off, it was because she was trying to manipulate me into an outcome. Subconsciously. I had to catch her when she did that and point it out to her.

"I can sense that you are trying to get an outcome with me right now."

You don't need to be aware of the many possible ways your woman could be manipulating you. Telling you all the specific things a woman could say to manipulate you would take up an entire book. Instead, a near foolproof way to know if your woman is manipulating you is to listen to your body. Your body tells you the truth, if you know how to listen to it. When your woman is manipulating you, you won't feel a strong urge to give to her motivated by joy. You will feel a resistance, an irritation, a lack of desire. That is a pretty good sign that you are probably being led in some way. And if what she is saying isn't directly leading you, that probably means she is covertly leading you. She is manipulating. Trust your body, and speak your truth about what you are sensing. She needs to know.

If you don't lead her to stop leading, you will end up resenting her. You will allow yourself to be manipulated, which means you will allow yourself to be led. You will subconsciously or consciously know that you are not in charge of the relationship, and it will destroy your desire to lead your woman with devotion. That will hurt both you and her.

You beat this level when you usually catch and call out your woman for manipulating you and she is receptive to working on stopping.

You get a perfect score when she no longer manipulates you.

DON'T LET HER 'TEACH' YOU

(LEVEL SEVEN)

A woman who argues with her man is trying to get an outcome. She is trying to make you believe something is true. She is trying to 'teach' you that you are wrong and she is right. She is trying to 'lead' you towards her way of thinking.

There is nothing wrong with a woman expressing her opinions. A woman should be encouraged to express her opinions respectfully. She should feel safe to do so. A woman needs to be able to express herself, and if you try to suppress her voice, it will hurt her and your relationship with her.

But there is a world of difference between expressing opinions and trying to teach opinions. When a woman expresses an opinion, she is not attached to the outcome of what she says. She is saying it because it is inside of her, and she just wants to share. She wants to express her internal world into the external world, for no reason other than because it feels good to express. Whereas when a woman teaches an opinion, she is trying to get you to believe what she believes. She is trying to get you to see her belief as right. She is trying to sway your views. She is trying to get an outcome.

The outcome she is trying to get by teaching may be selfless or selfish. She might be doing it to help you become better and smarter. Or she might be doing it for approval or to remain in control or to get her needs met. But the reason ultimately does not matter. Whatever the reason is, she is trying to lead you to an outcome, and so you must put a stop to it. If you don't, it will destroy your desire to connect with her and devote to her. You making her aware of what she is doing is a gift to her.

It's not only a gift because you are preventing her from impairing the relationship. It is also a gift because when she teaches you, she is draining her energy. It can be very energizing for a man to teach his woman. But it is draining for a woman to teach her man. She may do it because she feels compelled to, but it is hurting her. You guiding her to express without trying to get an outcome will help her, even if she doesn't realize it. It is energizing for a woman to express just to express. Lead her to do that.

"You are trying to teach me right now. Don't do that."

Your woman may resist your leadership. She may not understand that you are actually giving her a gift. It may help her if you explain why you do not want her to teach you. And reassure her that you do want to hear her opinions.

"I want to hear your opinion, but right now you are trying to teach me your opinion instead of express it. I am not interested in that."

She might still resist. It might even make her quite angry. If she continues to teach you, do not engage. Do not respond. Set a boundary for yourself that you will not argue with your woman, and you will not be a student of your woman. Don't engage. Don't be dismissive either. Don't ignore her rudely. Just continue to look at her with the expectation that she needs to stop before you are going to engage. This is not done to punish her! This is done because you love her. And she is hurting herself by continuing to teach, and you will hurt her further still if you enable it.

Teaching should only occur in one direction in a relationship; from you to her. That isn't because you are smarter or more wise and a woman has nothing to teach a man. It's because it's a man's job to lead to get an outcome by leading everything, and that means teaching. It's a woman's job to express without trying to get an outcome. That means not trying to teach. A woman will certainly teach a man many things in a relationship, but not by *trying* to teach him.

My wife has taught me so much in my relationship. I would not be the man I am today without her. I have learned so much about what it means to be responsible and to be considerate of another person. I have learned so much about how she thinks and how she views the world in a way that is quite different than me, but just as wonderful and valid. I have learned so much about people, psychology, relationships, and more from her. But I have only ever enjoyed it when she wasn't trying to teach it to me.

One of the reasons I chose my wife is because she was an intellectual. She is incredibly intelligent, and very knowledgeable about many topics. I used to derive a lot of enjoyment from debating with her. But now I enjoy no enjoyment from it. The reason why is because I am fully devoted to her. All I want to do is make her life better by giving her all of my best gifts. Those gifts include my gift of knowledge. Whenever my wife debates me on anything I say, she is rejecting my gift. She is resisting it, and saying she doesn't value it. A woman debating with a man is insulting his gift that he is offering. That's why I won't engage anymore if she tries. I love hearing her opinions, but not when she is *trying* to *teach* me those opinions.

When a woman starts teaching a man her opinions, it will often lead to more than an intellectual debate. It will turn into an argument. This is where the debate shifts from both man and woman trying to teach about the world, to trying to teach about each other's behaviors and intent. It becomes personal.

"You are being selfish."

"That is very rude."

"What you are doing is abusive."

"You are always doing that."

A man doesn't want to be taught by his woman, and he definitely does not want to be taught about his behaviors. If your woman does this to you, you will notice yourself likely becoming defensive and disagreeing, even when you can see deep down that she is right. The problem isn't that she is right, the problem is that she is trying to teach you that she is right. She is trying to lead you to that conclusion. And you disagreeing is your way of resisting that teaching. It's not a particularly mature way of doing it, and unfortunately your woman will start to believe that you are incapable of accepting responsibility for anything.

But a man is usually capable of accepting responsibility, only if that responsibility is not taught to him. You don't want to be led, so stop your woman from trying to teach you your responsibility. Lead her to express how your behavior makes her feel.

"You are trying to teach me right now. I do not care what you think of my behaviors. If you have a problem with me, I need you to tell me how you feel. What are you feeling right now?"

Lead her to express herself to you in an "I feel" statement.

"I feel sad."

"I feel irritation."

"I feel anger."

Now you can lead by asking her why she feels that way. Obviously you don't want her to feel that way, and if you did something inappropriate to trigger that emotional response, you will want to take responsibility for that behavior. Lead her to only express what behavior you were exhibiting to cause that reaction, don't let her judge the behavior, and don't let her make assumptions about the behavior. If she does then she is back to teaching you about your behavior.

"Because I don't get to go on dates with you anymore."

"Because I'm not getting attention when I was trying to tell you something."

"Because you were raising your voice at me."

Now she isn't leading, she is just expressing the problem. You now have an opportunity to accept responsibility for your actions and work on yourself if it was a problem. You changing your own behaviors to make her happy can now be done as a gift to her, rather than a burden she puts on you. If she tries to lead you in any way, it will feel like a burden for you to change. But if she doesn't lead you and only expresses, you are energetically free to change through your own leadership, instead of submitting to hers.

Arguments get kicked up a notch when a woman starts blaming a man. And usually when a woman gets into teaching mode, there is an element of blame attached to her words. A woman who blames a man is leading. Blame happens when a woman's beliefs get attacked in some way. She is receiving contradictory evidence that her beliefs are true, and that creates cognitive dissonance. To remove the cognitive dissonance and repair the damage to her belief, she needs to negate the contradictory evidence. If her man gave her the contradictory evidence, then the way to negate it is by making him into the bad guy. She does this by 'blaming' him, which is an energetic attack.

My wife is most likely to blame me when I do something that makes her feel disrespected. This is never intentional and always innocent on my part, because I would never want to make her feel that way on purpose. One of the best examples of this was when I was first teaching her how to communicate to me without leading to get an outcome. She was trying, but wasn't doing the best job. I tried correcting her, and she felt disrespected. When a person feels disrespected, it means that their belief about being worthy of respect has been attacked. In their minds, if they truly were worthy of respect, they would not have received something that they perceive as disrespect.

My wife blamed me for this by getting angry at me and telling me that I was 'being disrespectful'. In her mind, she was trying to make me out as trying to hurt her. If she could have convinced herself and me that I was trying to hurt her, then she could have repaired her belief that she was worthy of respect. She would then believe that she is was still worthy of respect, but that I was just a disrespectful person. It's no longer about her, it's about me. This is perhaps the most dangerous and destructive form of leading because it is very subconscious, and so it isn't immediately apparent. But it is leading, because the woman is trying to get the outcome of convincing her man of something by energetically forcing him to accept the blame.

My wife felt disrespected, and she did not want to be responsible for that feeling, so she tried to convince me that I am disrespectful by blaming me. The problem was I didn't want to take the blame, and no man does. I was not going to be convinced that my behavior was disrespectful or that I am a disrespectful person, because those things were untrue. Nor am I going to accept responsibility for her feelings when her feelings are her responsibility. I choose to be responsible for her happiness, but I do so as a gift. If she blames me for making her unhappy, she is making my gift into an obligation.

I explained this to my wife. But if your woman is angry, this is where arguing gets out of control. She won't want you to lead her to accept the actual truth. She will resist and blame even more, because your truth is just more contradictory evidence to her beliefs.

And if her blame attacks also trigger you into blaming back, you are now in a real mess. And as the man, you are responsible for leading both of you out of that mess. Any conflict is your job to lead to resolution. And the best way to do that is usually to lead your woman to take responsibility for her feelings by asking her how she feels.

"How do you feel right now?"

This often can get her out of her head where she is rationalizing why you are wrong, and into her body, where she can feel and process her pain. If she is receptive to expressing her feelings, you can get her to elaborate and understand why she feels that way. You can get her out of attack mode (trying to get an outcome), and into expressing mode (not trying to get an outcome).

If you continue to feel her blame as she tries to convince you, you can very calmly let her know that you would really like to know more about this and hear what she has to say, but you aren't going to listen if she is going to blame you. If she still isn't receptive, just stare at her and don't say anything until she starts following your lead. Don't react. If she doesn't follow your lead after giving her a good window of opportunity, leave. But whatever you do, do not continue arguing with her and escalating the situation. She needs to learn that she either takes responsibility for her feelings, or you are not going to engage. You are not going to let her teach you, especially not with blame based attacks.

You beat this level when you usually correct your woman when she is leading or blaming and she is receptive to changing.

You get a perfect score when your woman no longer leads or blames.

DON'T LET HER SET BOUNDARIES
(LEVEL EIGHT)

***Disclaimer: If you aren't EXTREMELY serious about leading in your woman's best interest, this chapter is definitely not for you. You need to grow up first before messing around with something as serious as your woman's boundaries. I'm not joking. You could do a woman a lot of harm if you are not ready to become fully responsible as a man. If you *are* ready to become that kind of responsible man, read on:

A woman who tries to enforce boundaries with a man is trying to lead him to stop behaving in a certain way. A boundary is any line that a woman draws between behavior she wants to accept and behavior she doesn't want to accept. Some boundaries are rigid and fixed, for example a woman should always have a boundary against being screamed at. Other boundaries are flexible and situation dependent, for example a woman who doesn't want to talk in a certain moment because she is busy. There are many boundaries a woman could be enforcing with her man on a day to day basis, and she will usually assert those boundaries with a "no", "don't", or "stop".

When a woman enforces boundaries with you, she is trying to assert her needs. Her need in that moment is for you to stop doing what you are doing because it is hurting her in some way. Or she perceives that it will hurt her in some way. She is trying to protect herself from harm, usually emotional harm. Sometimes (usually) this is very insignificant harm. This could be something really small such as you saying "Hey come here." because you wanted to kiss her or tell her something and she says "No." In this case the 'harm' would be very mild inconvenience if she didn't want to do it. Or it could be something huge like you leading her to do a sexual act she is extremely uncomfortable with due to past trauma, and she says "No". In this case the 'harm' could be enormous such as creating further trauma and huge trust issues.

Here are some of the things I have done in my relationship where my wife would enforce a boundary by saying "no", "don't", or "stop":

When I told her to come over and sit with me.

When I would walk over to kiss her.

When I would try taking her clothes off to have sex with her.

When I would touch her and it was ticklish or felt uncomfortable.

When I told her I wanted her to communicate without trying to get an outcome...

It is an extremely long list. My wife has no problem whatsoever about enforcing boundaries. Whenever she didn't want what I was giving or offering for whatever reason, she would assert a boundary. And every time, I felt a little bothered by it, but didn't understand why. But there is a very good reason why:

When a woman enforces boundaries with her man, she is preventing him from fully being the leader he could be. She is preventing him from being able to be completely devotional with her. That act also means that she is preventing herself from being able to fully let go and trust her man. She isn't able to fully submit to a man's leadership until she stops trying to enforce her boundaries with him. This means that a woman's boundaries are in the way of having a perfect relationship. The more 'no's she is giving her man throughout the day, the more imperfect the relationship will be.

A woman certainly has the right to enforce her boundaries if she wants to do so. It is her time, her energy, her body, her possessions, her life. So it is her choice to make boundaries to defend herself against you. Or is it?

The answer is actually 'no'. You should not tolerate your woman enforcing boundaries with you in a devotional relationship. When she tries to enforce boundaries with you by telling you to do something or not do something, what she is doing is communicating that she does not trust you or respect you as the leader. You need to put a stop to that.

On the surface, it sounds so obvious that of course she should be able to enforce her boundaries. But what if you have a boundary against being led by your woman? Why is it a violation if you raise your voice at your woman, but it's not a violation of your boundary when she leads you? It hurts a woman when you yell. And it hurts you when your woman leads. It's disrespectful when you yell. It is disrespectful when she leads. So whose boundary wins out?

Yours should, because you are the man, and you should be leading everything in the relationship. That is your expectation you should be setting, and your woman is free to follow that expectation or leave the relationship. Your woman always has the right to enforce her boundaries because she is a sovereign individual. But in *your* relationship, you make the expectations, and you give her the choice to stick around and work towards submitting to those expectations, or not.

Choice is a very important word. You should never *force* your woman to submit to your expectations. If you have a boundary against being led, and she has boundaries she wants to enforce by leading you, you can't force her to stop leading you. You want your woman to submit to you in every way possible, but it must be for the right reasons. It should never be through energetic force. It should never be through fear. It should be through loving respect to you as the man of the relationship. You need to make it clear that you have a boundary against her leading you, and you need to make her understand why it is important to you. The best way to do this is situation dependent. You know your woman better than I do. But there is a way. The more work you have done on the other levels, the easier it will be to get through to your woman on this.

More importantly, you need to make her understand why it is in her best interest to submit to your boundary, and why she is safe to do so. This can be a difficult task because boundaries are a sensitive topic, especially for any woman whose boundaries have been violated by someone who was supposed to protect her. This may have caused enormous trauma for a woman which she will guard against by creating very strong, and often very unnecessary boundaries. This deserves compassion and understanding from a man. It requires the ability to be patient and considerate of her feelings. There will be a lot of fear surrounding her boundaries, and you cannot lead her to stop enforcing boundaries more quickly than she is ready for. You have to be flexible in your boundaries for a while as you lead her increasingly to letting go of enforcing hers. There is a reason that stopping your woman from making boundaries is the 'final level'. It's because with many women it is extremely *hard.* And if there was anything that you do not want to screw up, it is your leadership surrounding her boundaries. Take this stuff extremely seriously.

To lead your woman to stop enforcing boundaries, you need to make it clear to her that you have an expectation of yourself that you do not hurt her feelings by violating her. Your chosen job in your relationship is to make your woman better off. You want to respect her and make her happy, and avoid making her feel hurt. You need to explain that you take her feelings extremely seriously, and all she needs to do is tell you how your behaviors or leadership is making her feel, and you will try very hard to lead based on those feelings. Make her understand that she doesn't need to assert herself to protect against your behaviors. She only needs to guide your leadership by being vulnerable so you can set your own boundaries to protect her... from yourself.

When she tells you "no", "stop", or "don't", tell her "Don't tell me what not to do, tell me how you feel."

When a woman expresses her feelings vulnerably, she is not asserting herself. When a woman asserts herself she is trying to change her environment is some way. She is trying to get someone to do something or stop doing something. That is not why a woman should express her feelings. She should not be trying to change her man's behaviors, because that implies a lack of trust in her man. She should only be trying to express how his behaviors are impacting her, and trust that her man will want to adjust his behaviors if he believes he is making her worse off. When a woman expresses her feelings she is not asserting a boundary. But her expressing a feeling potentially indicates where a boundary may be.

"I feel sad."

"I feel anxious."

"I feel discomfort."

If you lead your woman to stop leading you with her boundaries, you need to be willing to grow up extremely fast. It will require you take a very hard look at yourself as a man. Are you an honorable man who cares about how your woman feels and wouldn't take advantage of her for any reason? If you aren't, you need to work on yourself. Because you have absolutely no authority to tell your woman to stop setting boundaries with you when you lack honor. You are not safe, and she absolutely should not trust you. That is why you need to make a commitment to act honorably, no matter what. You need to decide that her feelings are far more important than your wants. You must take her trust extremely seriously and act responsibly. Not just by acting with honorable intent, but also by acting competently enough to not hurt her with your decisions.

This is the process that I went through as a man. I love testing boundaries. Playfully. It is fun for me. It is a game. But it is a game for boys, not for men. A man doesn't test a woman's boundaries. He creates his own boundaries to protect her from himself. So that she doesn't have to enforce her own. I realized that I would have to completely stop testing boundaries if I was going to grow up as a man. I started taking my wife's feelings extremely seriously. If she said she was feeling irritated or uncomfortable because of something I was doing, I would stop doing it. If I didn't begin taking her feelings very seriously, my wife would never have started to trust me to stop enforcing her boundaries herself.

When I told her to stop enforcing her boundaries, she at first thought it was outrageous, because without a ton of context and explanation, it does sound outrageous. And it sounds incredibly dangerous and toxic. I was persistent, because I knew this was a very important aspect of a healthy relationship. She eventually began consciously not setting boundaries, and instead just telling me how she felt. It wasn't easy for her. She has a need to feel in control, and a need to be perceived as strong. So to let go of control and also be vulnerable was a very big deal. I felt very respected that she would do that for me, and I tried very hard to not let her down.

Now I act as my wife's protector in our relationship. I am always thinking about her feelings, and I am always thinking of ways that I can keep her safe and comfortable. It is second nature to me. I used to only focus on myself. My own needs and my own boundaries. But now I am hyper-vigilant because I am focused on her feelings. I always want to make her feel good, and I want to avoid making her feel bad. And I want her to trust me completely. I have created strong inner boundaries for my own behavior to make sure I succeed in that goal.

You should have a similar goal. Your goal is to make your woman trust you completely. Fully. Deeply. On all levels. You want her to be willing to do whatever you say. The reason you have that goal should not be because you have a sick perverted cult leader personality and can't wait to do what you want with her. That would be incredibly irresponsible. You want her trust so that you can give as much to her as possible. With full trust, you can make the best possible decisions for her and give her gifts that will benefit her but that she might initially be resistant to.

A woman's trust is not something you should take lightly. It is a deep honor to be trusted fully as a man. If you abuse that trust, you are unlikely to get it back easily, if at all. By losing her trust, you will hurt her and hurt the relationship, significantly. Treat her trust like it is a priceless delicate gift, because it is.

If you are leading your woman to do something that makes her feel extremely uncomfortable and she tells you so, that is usually a good reason to back off. Because you don't want her to feel that way. You aren't backing off because she is assertively telling you to. You are backing off because you are devoted to her heart. The reason is now completely different. Instead of not doing something because she isn't allowing you to do it, you aren't doing something because you aren't allowing yourself to do it. Your responsibility is to develop inner boundaries for your own behavior. These boundaries are based on your honor; a set of principles that you use to determine right from wrong.

"Am I making my relationship better off or worse off by doing something?"

If you discern that you would be making the relationship worse off by doing something, then don't do it. That includes discerning that you will lose some of her trust if you choose to do something that is hurting her.

But if you discern that you would be making the relationship better by doing something, then do it. You should not always choose to not do something just because your woman says she feels uncomfortable, scared, or sad. Sometimes it is still the right thing to do. If you always led based on your woman's feelings, she would never grow out of her comfort zone. She would never heal out of her traumas. She would never be able to experience your best gifts that you can give her. Her boundaries are often stopping her from experiencing hurt. But some are preventing her from experiencing pleasure. And some are preventing her from healing trauma. If you are a very competent leader, you will be able to usually discern the difference and lead in her best interest.

If you discern that you will make the relationship better off by doing something, and it turns out you were wrong and hurt your woman, you need to be ready to take responsibility for that. If your woman is going to let go and trust your judgment and decisions, that means you are now fully responsible for those decisions. Her only responsibility is to express how that decision makes her feel, before and after it is done. You are responsible for deciding to take those feelings into account or not when making that decision. If you choose to go through with the decision, and it hurts her, that's your responsibility.

If you choose to make excuses for your decision, you are being irresponsible.

If you choose to blame her for being hurt, you are being irresponsible.

If you choose to ignore or downplay the outcome, you are being irresponsible.

If you choose to tell her she shouldn't feel that way, you are being irresponsible.

The only responsible thing to do in that situation is tell her you made a mistake in your judgment and that you are sorry you hurt her. If necessary, do something to make it up to her. If you don't, you will begin losing her trust. She cannot feel comfortable submitting to a man's leadership if he is unwilling to own his mistakes. A woman can be very forgiving of a man who owns his mistakes and takes responsibility for making them. She knows that no man is perfect, and no man will always make the right decision. She can let go of those mistakes because she knows that a responsible man can learn from them and do better next time. She will be much less forgiving if a man proves that he is irresponsible, because irresponsible men don't learn from their mistakes. They put the responsibility onto someone or something else to protect their own ego, and continue to repeat the error. Such men are not safe. Do not be that type of man. Your woman deserves much better from you.

As a 'fail safe' to ensure you do not accidentally violate your woman in a way that will deeply hurt her, you should also teach her what she *should* do if you continue to lead her to do something she is truly not comfortable with and isn't willing to do. Tell her that if she has expressed her feelings and is feeling increasingly unheard and uncomfortable, she should tell you something like:

"I feel really angry right now and I need to be by myself with my feelings."

And then she should walk away.

If she tells you this, she isn't leading. She isn't telling you to do something or not do something. She isn't saying 'no', 'don't' or 'stop'. But she is telling you that you are trying to lead her past a boundary that she is not willing to cross. This is your cue to back way off.

Teaching her this method of expressing her boundary without leading you is a huge gift that every woman needs. You can do a lot of emotional damage to a woman if you lead her to stop enforcing any of her boundaries and just express how she feels, and you then push past a boundary she is not willing to let go of because you think it will be in her best interest. Even if you end up being right, you will still be wrong, because the violation itself will do her harm, and do your relationship harm. That is why she needs to know that she always has the choice to walk away. Submission is always a choice, and you need to make it clear to her that she has that choice with you. You aren't teaching her that she isn't allowed to have boundaries, you are teaching her that she's not allowed to enforce them with you by leading *you*.

If she submits to your leadership for the wrong reasons, that isn't a gift you are giving her, that is subjugation. You are leading her into deeper levels of submission because you you want to give her even more gifts, not to subjugate her. She must understand that she always has the right to walk away from any situation where she is feeling very uncomfortable. You are not a controlling man, you are a devoted man. So make it clear she has that choice if she isn't already fully aware of it.

You beat this level when you usually tell your woman to stop enforcing her boundaries when she tries and she is receptive to expressing her feelings. And you are competent at leading based on her feelings.

You get a perfect score when your woman has total trust in you that you will lead in her best interest and she submits to what you say even if it makes her uncomfortable or scared... And you *never* give her any reason for her trust in your leadership to waver.

CONCLUSION
(YOU WIN THE GAME!)

You now know the eight levels of the game 'Don't Let Her Lead'. You also know the strategy to beat each level and win the game.

Now it is a matter of actually playing the game with your woman and winning with her.

That is easier said than done. It is scary to lead. It can even be terrifying. When a man leads, he risks rejection, he risks judgment, he risks ridicule, and he risks failure. He doesn't know how his woman will respond.

This fear is even worse when the man is fully heart open and leading out of devotion. Everything in this book should ideally be accomplished by doing it *for* your woman. By energetically giving her a gift of your boundaries and leadership. And when your heart open leadership is rejected or judged or ridiculed, it hurts a lot more. Which means your mind will try to protect you more by scaring you away from doing it.

Do it anyway.

Do not let any fear stop you from beating the game. The best way to do that is to actually treat it like a game. A game that you really want to win and take deadly seriously. But also one that you know is just a game, it's not life and death.

When you take games seriously, you end up having a lot more fun playing them. You end up putting in all of your effort, and when you try your best, it's more enjoyable than just messing around.

But if it doesn't go the way as planned, there is no need to throw the controller through the television. Because it is just a game, and you can try again to beat a level.

Take the same approach with your relationship. Approaching relationship development as a game is important because it helps a man become more patient and understanding. If he takes this work too seriously, he may become very needy and impatient for results. This can lead to controlling and even angry reactions when his woman doesn't respond 'the way she is supposed to'. If you do that, she is only going to become more resistant to doing what you want. That is why you should try your hardest, but recognize it is not the end of the world if you don't win right away. If you get angry at your woman because she is making things difficult, don't take that anger out on her. Maintain self control and invent a way to beat the level. Remember, she's on your team, even when she isn't acting like it.

Your woman is supposed to react however she reacts, and you need to figure out a solution to lead her better. You can't force her to stop leading, and you shouldn't try. She is leading because of trauma. And the way to help her heal trauma is with love, not with force. That is why you must see this as a fun game. You try hard, but you don't freak out when you don't get the results you were hoping for. It may take time. Sometimes results happen right away. But it big results may take months of consistent effort.

Getting as far as I have in my relationship was not easy. It required pushing through a lot of resistance and judgment from my wife. There were hurt feelings on both sides. There were times I had to temporarily let go of my inner-vision by watering it down, because she wasn't ready for what I was offering. It was a really tough sell. It has become an increasingly easy one the further we get.

But I don't think we ever would have made it this far if I took my relationship goals too seriously and tried to force them on her. I am serious about my goals. I am determined and persistent to attain them. I also do not act like this is life and death. This is fun for me, and getting as far as I want to go will take as long as it takes. In the meantime, my relationship has become amazing for both my wife and I because I work very hard and don't let her lead. And she works very hard at not leading.

This is a journey that I am still on. Every man still is, because there is always more work to be done to improve your relationship and yourself further. To become even more solid as a devoted masculine man. More grounded. More centered. More focused. More loving. More powerful.

I work every day to become a better man for my wife. To catch her in all the subtle ways she still tries to lead, and help her with letting go of control. While simultaneously becoming a better leader so that she feels no urge to lead. It's really fun and enjoyable. I have beaten all of the levels on easy mode. It took less than a year. It should take less than a year for you too. Probably much less than that if you take it really seriously. I had to figure it out by trial and error. But you have my book!

Now I am working on my perfect score. That will take much longer. It might even be impossible in this lifetime. But I'm going to try my best anyway, because there is nothing that could possibly be more fun than trying. I see it as the best game I could ever play. And I get to play it with the woman I love most in the world.

Play your own game with your woman and win it together. Start today.

You can take what you've learned here and start making some amazing shifts. However, making these shifts will not be easy. In fact, it will almost certainly be the hardest thing you ever do. Even if you now have a general idea of what you need to do. There's a few reasons for that.

1. It's very uncomfortable. Taking control as a man may go against all of your learned survival patterns. The level of discomfort and number of excuses you make to stay stuck will keep you avoiding what you really need to do.

2. It's very painful. On this journey you will be judged. Your needs will often not be met. This process will also take far longer than you likely anticipate. When you don't get the responses you want, the pain and stories you tell yourself will compel you into giving up.

3. You will make tons of mistakes. I've outlined the basics in this book to get you started and give you a fantastic overview of how to create the dream relationship and shift your communication. But there is a steep learning curve and the only way to get what you want and need is to make thousands of mistakes along the way.

4. You won't know how to communicate in every situation, nor will you know how to lead a woman to communicate in every situation. There is far more depth to this work than what I have outlined here. I'd need to write a thousand books of this size to fully convey the depth and breadth of communicating as a man and woman. While it is theoretically possible to figure it all out by trial and error like a good social scientist, the three points above are going to make that far more challenging than it needs to be.

I do have solutions for these problems though, because I want to make this journey as easy as I can for you.

SOLUTION 1: Join our facebook group. With over 10,000 members, you get to be part of a huge community who are learning from my books and teachings. It's FREE.

SOLUTION 2: Read all of my other books. They all contain different pieces of the puzzle to make these shifts easier for you. Yes, they are marketed to women, but guess what, to be a good leader, you need to learn how to better teach her. Those books will help you be a better man. The more you understand conceptually, the less mistakes you will make and the less likely you will be to give up.

SOLUTION 3: Join our 2 hour Polarized Communication Masterclass. We don't just talk about masculine and feminine communication, we demonstrate it in live roleplays. You also get to ask us questions. Seeing this in action will supercharge your understanding of what this looks like energetically and it will be a powerful belief shifting experience.

SOLUTION 4: The first three solutions are easily affordable (or in the case of the group, free). But if you know you want real expert support at helping you make these shifts, join us in my group program for men and for women; 'Relationship Of Your Dreams Academy'. This is where you will get all of the video content you need to understand what and how to shift on a far deeper level. You will get a group of hundreds of dedicated clients to ask questions, have this communication role modelled, and practice communicating in a safe supportive container. You will also get one on one and group roleplay calls where we will roleplay any relevant situations to show you how to make these shifts and lovingly correct you when you misapply the teachings.

The Academy is focused on giving you the space to practice and refine your communication and learn to receive, while we support you in your journey. We help you move through your pain, your fears, your stories, and your many inevitable mistakes. We take you on a journey from understanding this work conceptually in your head, to understanding it and shifting it in your body. We facilitate your embodiment.

The Academy is more than a coaching program. It's a family. My family, that I created.

Working with us doesn't mean we can take your fear away or make this journey painless. That would be impossible. But we can take you by the hand and make it a lot easier for you.

We can decrease the amount of time that these shifts would

take. The same progress you would make in many years to a decade could be made in a matter of months or up to a year. We will help you through all of your fears, and self-sabotage, and make this considerably less painful, and significantly more fun than it would be alone.

It's possible to do it all yourself. I would never lie to you and say it isn't. But you'll be paying a very heavy price in time and an unnecessary degree of painful feelings." After all, if you're a mountain climber, you could climb Mt. Everest by yourself. But with a competent team of sherpas who've got your back and show you the way with their decades of expertise, why would you attempt Mt. Everest by yourself? It would be lonely, cold and potentially deadly.

We have helped facilitate the transformations of so many men and women so that they could create the relationship of their dreams. I'd love it if you were one of the next ones.

To access any or all of the four solutions presented, go to www.relationshipofyourdreams.com

You can try to play this game on hard mode, but why do that when there is further help I can offer you to make it much easier and fun?

.... One last thing. I would be incredibly grateful if you did me favor to fulfill my purpose in helping people transform their relationships: If you found this book helpful, please take two minutes to write a quick review on Amazon. Tell all of your friends to get the book too.

Thankyou for reading.

Made in the USA
Coppell, TX
24 November 2024

40941453R00049